CHIHULY | PERSIANS

C H I H U L Y | P E R S I A N S

Curated by Henry Geldzahler

Dia Art Foundation
Bridgehampton, NY

July 10-August 21, 1988

Working photos 1988 by Ray Charles White

Foreword

Henry Geldzahler

The first image that comes to mind when we attempt to describe Dale Chihuly's work and his trajectory through life is one of fluid movement with elusively infected highlights. His life, largely spent on the road, is dictated by his prime obsessions, the making of glass and the conditions of exhibiting it. In recent years he has come to the conclusion that his task does not end when the glass has been blown and allowed to cool. Photographing the work and designing simple, effective installations are necessary stages in communicating with his audience.

The delightful thing about much new art of quality is its mischievous ability to break the rules. Chihuly successfully resists being trapped in many of the pigeonholes that make for neat categories, but leach art of its complexity. First, he confidently bestrides the distinction between craft and art. And second, he has never felt the need to choose between abstraction and representation — between the natural and the invented — which has proven the great bugaboo in art all these years.

This issue of art vs. craft has been rearing its head in American art in the past decade. Artists as diverse as Kenneth Price and Peter Voulkos in ceramic, Wendell Castle in wood, and Dale Chihuly in glass have crossed the Rubicon, never to step backward into the medieval guild. The blurring of art categories is one of the bequests of the radicalism of the 1960's that these artists have effected and benefited from. Old distinctions between "fine" and "decorative" art, between the "uselessness" of high art and the "usefulness" of furniture, vessels, and porcelain no longer have meaning for us. They have taken their place with the "impossible" conflicts of previous generations: Romantic vs. Classic, Sacred vs. Profane.

What is the "use" of a Dale Chihuly sculpture? (Note how easily "sculpture" and not "piece of glass" slips into our discussion.) It locates the magic and alchemy inherent in molten glass, in gorgeous and permanent materiality. His work stands for change in constancy, highlights on surfaces of permanent fluidity, which cannot help but serve as an ethical standard for anyone who lives with it. One may put oranges or limes in his "baskets" or dried flowers in his "cylinders," but then one can also use a Picasso to cover a hole in the wall.

From *Chihuly; Color Glass and Form* published by Kodansha International Ltd. 1986

Dale Chihuly's

Persians:

Acts of Survival

Robert Hobbs

In his elegant yet strangely disturbing series of *Persians*, Dale Chihuly courts the miraculous. Each element making up the *Persians* is intensely conceived: The pieces combine the delicacy of threaded Venetian glass, which Chihuly learned in 1968 in Murano, Italy, with the distinctive woven patterns that are the hallmark of his *Baskets* and *Sea Forms*. But unlike these earlier series, which are compact displays of fecund shapes that appear ready to propagate still other forms, the *Persians* suggest found treasure. They call to mind the mysterious clusters of ancient Greek pots in Etruscan tombs that have survived grave robbers, or the haunting juxtapositions of remnants of standing walls, overturned columns, and rubble that characterize ancient ruins. The compositions of the *Persians* look as if they occurred by happenstance, while the fragility of glass itself lends a special poignancy to these pieces because they appear to have survived time and pillaging.

The individual elements in the *Persians* still exude life. The elasticity of each form manifests glass's real character as a frozen liquid, as molecules held in suspension. And the life force imbuing Chihuly's art makes it sculpture rather than mere bibelots. The individual elements composing the *Persians* simulate the rhythms and forces of life: Their variously shaped orifices are dilated; the necks of bottles, which resemble ancient perfume containers, stretch forth with wonderous elasticity; and huge *tazzas*, still attached to the glass stems, which held them to pontil rods while they were being formed, have gracefully succumbed to gravity, and consequently lean, twist, and turn. The pontil stems not only point to process — a concept of great importance to many modern artists — but they also emphasize the original centers of the individual pieces before the gaffer and Chihuly, in the last stage of creating them, deflected their course and made them acknowledge gravity's force. The pontil stem, then, underscores the internal tensions in each of these individual pieces, which have dramatically turned away from their original centers. The *Persians* are less related to abundant still lifes in the manner of the *Sea Forms* and more akin to casually displayed shards of ancient cultures that exude the life of distant times and places. Precariousness is underscored in some *Persians* that droop over the edges of pedestals and in others where pieces propped against each other contrast with isolated, delicate bottles that stand miraculously erect.

Mars Red and Winsor Green Persian Pair
1988
19″ x 17″ x 22″
Photograph by Dick Busher

7

For some time Dale Chihuly has been fascinated with ancient glass. Unlike Louis Comfort Tiffany, who earlier in this century attempted to recreate the patina of time in his Favrile glass that was shaped to resemble water lilies and trailing vines, Chihuly does not attempt to make the surfaces of his pieces appear weathered and, therefore, ancient. Rather, he goes back to certain Near Eastern forms that he then pulls out of shape, so that they look as if they had been transformed by some immanent force. Chihuly does not use the colors of ancient glass, even though the new oxbloods and opalescent whites in which he originally conceived the series suggest an exotic world, an ambiance that is reinforced in other pieces in the series by intense blues, chrome yellows, and oranges.

The *Persians* were made in a new workshop called the "glass lab" that Chihuly established last year not far from his Buffalo Studio near Seattle's downtown. He set up the glass lab so that he could work on a regular basis with a small crew and not be totally dependent on the larger team that he pulls together several times a year at Pilchuck, the Rhode Island School of Design, or at the studios of other glassblowers, such as that of his former teacher Harvey Littleton. The smaller workshop, with its full-time crew under the direction of gaffer Martin Blank, has given Chihuly the opportunity and flexibility to experiment freely, and the *Persians*, which are generally smaller and more densely decorated than any prior series, are the result of this experimentation. Chihuly has been able to indulge his fascination with elaborate threading patterns to create basket weaves, waffled designs, and combed decorations. Some of the individual pieces making up the *Persians* look almost like Waterford cut glass, so intense are the waffled designs, even though relief cutting has never been part of Chihuly's repertoire.

To name a series "Persian" at this time could suggest a reference to certain political realities. This title provides an important frame for the series; it imbues it with the romance of ancient Persia, which Iran's new Islamic Republic is now rejecting. Chihuly's loosely assembled pieces of glass suggest the precarious position of Persian culture in the modern world. "Persia" connotes a special and distant realm of refinement and luxury, a place where mathematics, calligraphy, walled gardens, rich carpets, mystical love poetry, and elaborately decorated, finely blown glass vessels were created and respected. Persia was located on the ancient silk route along which caravans traveled to and from China with spices, porcelain, silk, and new ideas. It was a crossroads between East and West, a seat of culture as well as a transmitter of concepts.

When Chihuly entitles a series "Persians," he draws upon a number of associations that refer to Persia as opposed to contemporary Iran. The delicacy and fragility of his glass as well as its tentative placement is an impression of this world: The series is like some wonderful perfume blown across the great central Iranian desert. The pieces allude to romance, mystery, an ancient world, and its survival in the present. These works may represent a new orientalism, but not idle exoticism or mere longing for the past, for there is a life force present, which overcomes any suggestion of blind nostalgia — their romantic sentiments exist as vital remnants of another time, as fragrant and significant scents of a great civilization's past flowering.

One might, however, still wonder if this reference to Persia is only exotic trimming for this artist who is a native of Tacoma, Washington. Could we not write off his endeavor as precious, as another case of a creative individual who is more in love with art than with life? Perhaps we could, except for the the fact that these pieces do manifest a healthy respect for the life force: They beguile and entrance and in the process convince us that they partake of a quality of life that we wish to understand more fully.

Chihuly's involvement with Persia might be more understandable if we look closely at his background and recognize that the poetic evocation of loss in the *Persians* has a parallel in his own life. During his teenage years, he experienced the profound difficulty of losing within a year-and-a-half both his older brother, who was training to become a pilot, and his father. These deaths impressed on him the precariousness of life and the need to hold onto the past and remember former pleasures. In his glass, this acceptance of life's fatal consequences is apparent in dilated openings, pulsating shapes, and forms acquiescing to the inevitability of gravity.

At this same time, Chihuly's mother had to assume new responsibilities, but she continued to tend their large flower garden, which abounded in lush and richly colored blossoms. The range of feelings Chihuly experienced about death, life, and the transitory but incredible beauty of flowers from his mother's garden is important to his art. In all of his work, balance is tentative, suggesting the precariousness of existence. This is true even when somewhat mitigated by the one or two large, comforting and enveloping forms that serve as "supports" for the *Baskets* and *Sea Forms*.

The interest in reclaiming and honoring the transient endows Chihuly's work with a special poignancy. In reaching beyond current harsh realities to the beauty that comes before — to the period in Middle Eastern civilization that manifested the living breath of culture — the artist's evocation of ancient Persia creates an aesthetic equivalent of his own life.

One can point to the Carpaccio painting of St. George and the Dragon in the Scuola degli Schiavoni, Venice, which Chihuly identifies as a source for the Persians, and say that the story and composition may serve as an organizing mythological principal for his series. The dragon may well symbolize recurring concerns about human loss, which are underscored in the painting by the dead bodies strewn across the landscape. Aspects of this dragon appear in some *Persians* in the spiky silhouettes that abstractly reiterate its wings. Like the painting, the *Persians* are both disturbing and yet exquisite, elegant yet emotionally moving.

Another personal point of reference that has a bearing on the *Persians* as well as on all of Chihuly's work is the artist's constant proximity to the sea. As a child, Chihuly was particularly close to the ocean. He and his family would go on outings where he collected sea shells, he saw grandiose views of the water daily en route to school, and he grew up with the idea that the sea was the great provider to the numerous fishing boats in the area. This positive feeling for the ocean is central to his overall compositions, which appear to be buoyed up by some invisible sea, and also to the individual forms comprising them. These forms seem to take on the convolutions of sea shells as well as the complex variegated colors of fish, shells, coral, and various underwater plants. Related to the ocean are the magnificent sunsets over the Tacoma bay, which are important to Chihuly's work. His preference for glowing, radiating colors no doubt develops out of the childhood ritual of regularly accompanying his mother to watch the setting sun.

All these environmental influences inform the *Persians*, but central to the series is the idea of retrieval. More than with any other works, including even the *Baskets*, which were inspired by a group of stacked and broken North American Indian baskets in a storeroom of the Washington State Historical Society, there is present the idea of reclamation. As mentioned earlier, most *Baskets* and *Sea Forms* are contained in generous bowls that hold carefully balanced elements and transform them into members of a family. But the elements making up the *Persians* do not form a reassuring whole. Although all the parts are related through intriguing interplays of color and texture, individual elements can be categorized as one of a number of clearly distinguished shapes. And added to this deliberate lack of unity is the way Chihuly has casually stacked and placed the various parts so that they appear unstable. In this way the artist establishes a new discordant tone to imply that the survival of the *Persians* is of greater importance than any overall unity they might manifest. One might say, then, that the *Sea Forms* and *Baskets* are concerned with an ecological balance, while the *Persians* are involved with preservation. The former group develops out of a single environment — they represent a single world view — while the latter bespeak of various currents and influences and exist at the crossroads of differing cultures and ideas.

In his new *Persians*, Chihuly gives voice to the accidental and serendipitous nature of life as against his earlier series that emphasized a cohesive life force. Existence, as the *Persians* suggest, is always tentative and precarious, always something to be fought and won... at least momentarily.

The author gratefully acknowledges conversations with Dale Chihuly, Viola Chihuly, Kate Elliott, and Robert Landsman. He deeply appreciates the careful and thoughtful reading of the essay by Raymond Foye, Henry Geldzahler, and Diana Johnson.

Saffron Stemmed Form with Royal Blue Persians
1988
23″ x 37″ x 23″
Photograph by Dick Busher

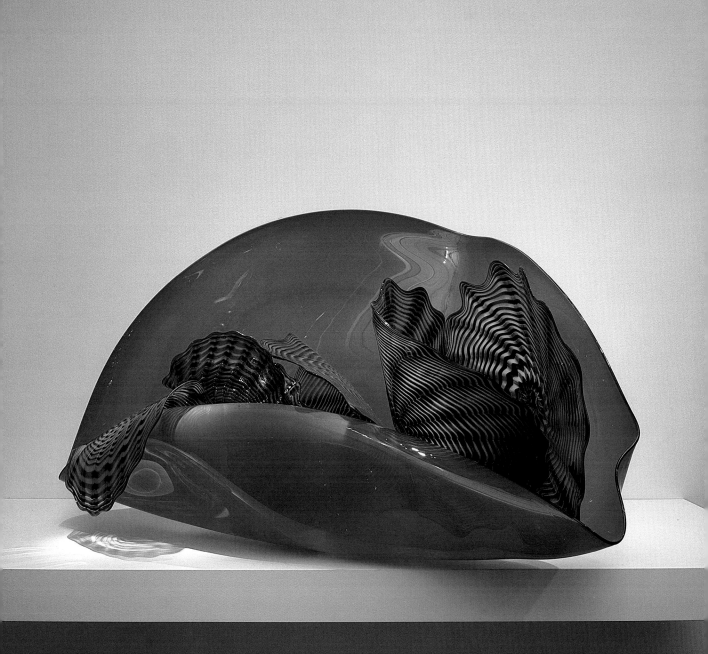

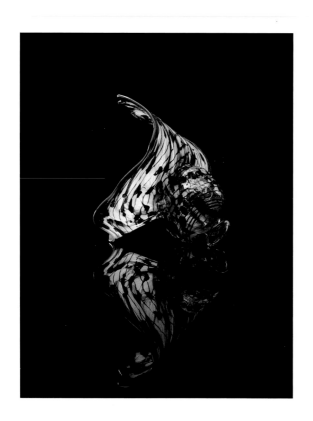

Early Persian Forms
1986
2"-7"
Photographs by Dick Busher

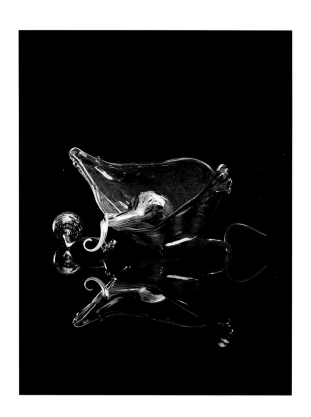

Rose Madder and Green Persian Shelf
1988
18½″ x 46″ x 20″
Photograph by Roger Schreiber

Drawing
1988
30″ x 22½″

Drawing

1988

30″ x 22½″

"When I start a new series of work, it is either a direct extension of what I was last making or abruptly different, or in the case of the *Persians,* can be in between. The individual forms are very different from previous forms, but the manner in which I put them together sometimes has the feeling of earlier groups of *Sea Forms.*"

"I've tried hundreds of different color combinations in the *Persians.* Lately I've been making very brightly colored little ones that go inside or alongside a large stemmed form. The stem was first developed to hold the bottom piece into a wall, but then I found that it also held the piece upright on a shelf in a nice way. The stem is the pontil and like an umbilical cord. Traditionally, that part of the piece was ground off, but I like to leave it on."

Lapis Stemmed Form with Orange Persians
1988
16" x 27" x 24"
Photograph by Roger Schreiber

Opaline Spined Sea Form with Cadmium Yellow Persians
1986
14″ x 25″ x 19″
Photographs by Dick Busher

Drawing
1988
30″ x 22½″

Drawing

1988

30″ x 22½″

"In 1977, I started the *Basket* series and became obsessed with the blowing process. Instead of using the traditional glass blowing tools, I began to use fire, gravity, centrifugal force, and chance to form the glass. I think this was the most important discovery I've made. I thought that it was the hot glass that was so mysterious, but then realized it was the air that went into it that was so miraculous. I often wonder how anyone ever thought of the idea of blowing air into molten glass. It doesn't work with any other materials."

Chrome Green Stemmed Form with Orange Persians
1988
15½″ x 22″ x 27″
Photograph by Roger Schreiber

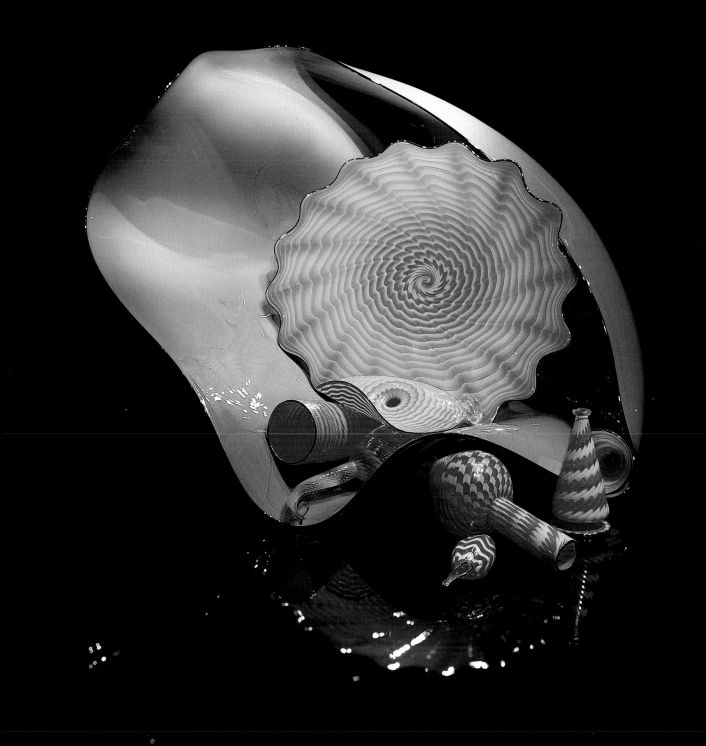

"Originally, I made the drawings so the gaffers could see and understand the forms I wanted them to blow. I started out wanting the drawings to look like the glass pieces so I experimented with different surface techniques which resulted in using bunches of graphite and colored pencils by the fistfuls. I would often draw on the steel marvering table with bits of glass under the paper to give it a texture. For color I used whatever I could find around the shop – tea, fruit juices, wine, coffee (my friend Italo's influence). I remember there was a period when I was drinking a lot of Seltzer with bitters – the bitters made a beautiful saffron color. Mecurochrome from the medicine kit also made a great orange, but the bouquet wasn't as good as the bitters."

Drawing
1988
30″ x 22½″

Chronology

1941   Born September 20 in Tacoma, Washington.

1960   Enters University of Washington, Seattle, in Interior Design and Architecture.

1961-62   Leaves school and sails for Europe and Middle East tour.

1962-64   Re-enters University of Washington, devoting much time to weaving. Begins experimentation with glass in tapestries.

1966-68   Earns money for graduate school as a commercial fisherman in Alaska. Receives MS from University of Wisconsin and MFA from Rhode Island School of Design in Providence. Concentrates on neon and environmental works. Meets Italo Scanga.

1968-69   Awarded Tiffany Grant and Fulbright Fellowship. The first American glass-blower to work at the Venini Glass Factory in Murano, Venice.

1971   Starts the Pilchuck Glass School with art patrons John Hauberg and Anne Gould Hauberg.

1976   Tours British Isles, loses sight in one eye in automobile accident. Henry Geldzahler purchases three *Navajo Blanket Cylinders* for the collection of the Metropolitan Museum of Art, New York.

1977-78   Begins *Pilchuck Baskets* which are shown at Seattle Art Museum in three-man show with James Carpenter and Italo Scanga curated by Charles Cowles. Exhibition of *Blanket Cylinders* and *Pilchuck Baskets* at Renwick Gallery, Smithsonian Institution, Washington, D.C.

1980   Resigns post as head of Glass Department at RISD, remaining as Artist-in-Residence. Begins developing *Sea Form* series.

1981-83   "Chihuly Glass" exhibition of *Sea Forms* organized by Kate Elliott to travel to five museums, accompanied by catalog written by Linda Norden.

1984   Works at Pilchuck preparing for "Chihuly: A Decade of Glass" which will tour fifteen museums under auspices of the Art Museum Association of America, accompanied by a catalog with essays by Karen S. Chambers and Jack Cowart.

1986   One-man show at the Musée des Arts Décoratifs, Paris featuring *Macchia* series tours Europe through 1989, accompanied by catalog with essays by Henry Geldzahler and Robert Hobbs. Kodansha publishes monograph *Chihuly: Color, Glass and Form* with essays by Karen S. Chambers, Dale Chihuly and Michael W. Monroe; foreword by Henry Geldzahler.

1987   Marries playwright Sylvia Peto. Completes sixty-foot long "Rainbow Flower Frieze" commission for Rockefeller Center.

1988   In March exhibits *Persians* for the first time at Charles Cowles Gallery, New York and Foster/White Gallery, Seattle concurrently.

Acknowledgement

My glass comes from teamwork, the efforts of a team of skilled glass blowers. I would like to thank all my friends from the gaffers to the photographers who made this exhibition possible. Without them this show would only be a dream.

Dale Chihuly
June 17, 1988
Seattle

Dia Art Foundation

155 Mercer Street
New York, NY 10012
212 431-9232

Charles B. Wright, *Executive Director*
Joan Duddy, *Assistant to the Director*
Gary Garrels, *Director of Programs*
Margaret Thatcher, *Administrator*

Corwith Avenue
P.O. Box 1286
Bridgehampton, NY 11932
516 537-1476

Henry Geldzahler, *Curator*
Saul Irving, *Gallery Assistant*

Frontispiece
Venetian Red and Lapis Persian Set with Red and Yellow Lip Wraps
1988
17″ x 28″ x 27″
Photograph by Roger Schreiber

Front and back covers
Experimental Persians
1986
1″-12″ long
Photographs by Dick Busher

Katy Homans, *Design*
Atomic Press, *Printing*
Thomas & Kennedy, *Typesetting*